TAPAS

MARKS &
SPENCER

TAPAS

SUSANNA TEE

Marks and Spencer p.l.c.
PO Box 3339, Chester CH99 9QS

T40/8283/0212C

www.marksandspencer.com

ISBN: 1-84461-026-8

Printed in China

Produced by the Bridgewater Book Company Ltd

Photographer: David Jordan

Home Economist: Jacqueline Bellefontaine

The views expressed in this book are those of the author but they are general views only and readers are urged to consult a relevant and qualified specialist for individual advice in particular situations. Marks and Spencer p.l.c. and Exclusive Editions Limited hereby exclude all liability to the extent permitted by law for any errors or omissions in this book and for any loss, damage or expense (whether direct or indirect) suffered by a third party relying on any information contained in this book.

Notes for the Reader

This book uses both metric and imperial measurements. Follow the same units of measurement throughout; do not mix metric and imperial. All spoon measurements are level: teaspoons are assumed to be 5 ml, and tablespoons are assumed to be 15 ml. Unless otherwise stated, milk is assumed to be full fat, eggs and individual vegetables such as potatoes are medium and pepper is freshly ground black pepper. Recipes using raw or very lightly cooked eggs should be avoided by infants, the elderly, pregnant women, convalescents and anyone suffering from an illness. The times given are an approximate guide only. Preparation times differ according to the techniques used by different people and the cooking times may also vary from those given. Optional ingredients, variations or serving suggestions have not been included in the calculations.

Picture acknowledgments
The Bridgewater Book Company would like to thank Corbis Images for permission to reproduce copyright material on pages 6, 8, 30, 52, 74.

CONTENTS

Small, irresistible mouthfuls of something savoury, served with a chilled white wine, beer or sherry – these are tapas, the national institution of Spain, eaten with enthusiasm in almost every bar before lunch and dinner.

The word tapa actually means lid, and comes from the slices of bread that the innkeeper would place on top of a person's wine glass to keep out the flies and dust between sips. The Andalucians then thought of the idea of balancing some kind of small food on top of this piece of bread, and tapas were born.

A full array of these tasty miniature morsels can make an informal lunch or dinner in themselves. For a meal, serve six to eight dishes, making your choice from a couple of recipes in each chapter. In addition, serve a selection of

INTRODUCTION

simple dishes, such as bowls of large olives and salted almonds, and accompany with a selection of salads.

Whatever your choice of recipes, tapas are for sharing and lingering over with a glass of something chilled. Eating tapas goes hand-in-hand with hospitality, friendship and lots of conversation. Enjoy the experience!

Just one bite means exactly that! Almost all tapas are no more than just a mouthful, but the recipes in this chapter really are literally only that — small, tasty morsels, served with a glass of chilled white wine, sherry or cold beer. It makes them the perfect partner to serve with pre-dinner drinks or at a drinks party, particularly as they are easy to pick up with your fingers. Highly flavoured and small, these appetizers whet your appetite but leave room for something else.

The simplest tapas dishes include a few slices of serrano ham or spicy chorizo sausage, a bowl of olives, cubes of Manchego cheese, olive oil-soaked garlic bread, artichoke hearts, fried prawns, anchovies or salted almonds. These

PART ONE
JUST ONE BITE

are the original tapas dishes that were offered along with a drink before they became more elaborate in a bid to attract customers. Recipes are hardly needed for some of these dishes, but this book gives you ideas for what to serve along with more substantial recipes.

Do provide cocktail sticks to spear these small delicacies and a saucer on which to discard the empty sticks! At some bars in Spain, the tapas are served on cocktail sticks and are known as pinchos. These all cost the same amount and, before a customer leaves, the waiter will count up the number of empty cocktail sticks to add to the bill. It is an inexpensive and enjoyable way of eating out.

CRACKED
MARINATED OLIVES

SERVES 8
as part of a tapas meal

450 g/1 lb can or jar
unstoned large green
olives, drained

4 garlic cloves, peeled

2 tsp coriander seeds

1 small lemon

4 sprigs of fresh thyme

4 feathery stalks of fennel

2 small fresh red chillies
(optional)

pepper

Spanish extra virgin olive
oil, to cover

To allow the flavours of the marinade to penetrate the olives, place on a chopping board and, using a rolling pin, bash them lightly so that they crack slightly. Alternatively, use a sharp knife to cut a lengthways slit in each olive as far as the stone. Using the flat side of a broad knife, lightly crush each garlic clove. Using a pestle and mortar, crack the coriander seeds. Cut the lemon, with its rind, into small chunks.

THE OLIVES WILL KEEP IN THE REFRIGERATOR FOR SEVERAL MONTHS, AND IN FACT THE LONGER YOU MARINATE THEM, THE MORE THEIR FLAVOUR WILL BE ENHANCED. USE THE OIL THAT THEY HAVE BEEN MARINATED IN EITHER FOR COOKING OR IN A SALAD DRESSING. IT WILL IMPART A DELICIOUS FLAVOUR TO A DISH.

Put the olives, garlic, coriander seeds, lemon chunks, thyme sprigs, fennel and chillies, if using, in a large bowl and toss together. Season with pepper to taste, but you should not need to add salt as conserved olives are usually salty enough. Pack the ingredients tightly into a glass jar with a lid. Pour in enough olive oil to cover the olives, then seal the jar tightly.

Leave the olives at room temperature for 24 hours, then marinate in the refrigerator for at least 1 week but preferably 2 weeks before serving. From time to time, gently give the jar a shake to re-mix the ingredients. Return the olives to room temperature and remove from the oil to serve. Provide cocktail sticks for spearing the olives.

SALTED ALMONDS

SERVES 6–8
as part of a tapas meal

225 g/8 oz whole
almonds, in their skins or
blanched (see method)

4 tbsp Spanish olive oil

coarse sea salt

1 tsp paprika or ground
cumin (optional)

Preheat the oven to 180°C/350°F/Gas Mark 4. Fresh almonds in their skins are superior in taste, but blanched almonds are much more convenient. If the almonds are not blanched, put them in a bowl, cover with boiling water for 3–4 minutes, then plunge them into cold water for 1 minute. Drain them well in a sieve, then slide off the skins between your fingers. Dry the almonds well on kitchen paper.

Put the olive oil in a roasting tin and swirl it around so that it covers the base. Add the almonds and toss them in the tin so that they are evenly coated in the oil, then spread them out in a single layer.

Roast the almonds in the oven for 20 minutes, or until they are light golden brown, tossing several times during the cooking. Drain the almonds on kitchen paper, then transfer them to a bowl.

While the almonds are still warm, sprinkle with plenty of sea salt and the paprika or cumin, if using, and toss well together to coat. Serve the almonds warm or cold. The almonds are at their best when served freshly cooked, so, if possible, cook them on the day that you plan to eat them. However, they can be stored in an airtight tin for up to 3 days.

ALMONDS ARE THE MOST POPULAR NUT TO BE SALTED AND SERVED AS A TAPA IN SPAIN, BUT HAZELNUTS ARE ALSO POPULAR AND CAN BE PREPARED IN EXACTLY THE SAME WAY. WALNUT HALVES, PISTACHIOS, PEANUTS AND CASHEWS COULD ALSO BE GIVEN THE SAME TREATMENT.

SAUTEED GARLIC MUSHROOMS

SERVES 6
as part of a tapas meal

450 g/1 lb button mushrooms

5 tbsp Spanish olive oil

2 garlic cloves, finely chopped

squeeze of lemon juice

salt and pepper

4 tbsp chopped fresh flat-leaved parsley

crusty bread, to serve

Wipe or brush clean the mushrooms, then trim off the stalks close to the caps. Cut any large mushrooms in half or into quarters. Heat the olive oil in a large, heavy-based frying pan, add the garlic and fry for 30 seconds–1 minute, or until lightly browned. Add the mushrooms and sauté over a high heat, stirring most of the time, until the mushrooms have absorbed all the oil in the pan.

Reduce the heat to low. When the juices have come out of the mushrooms, increase the heat again and sauté for 4–5 minutes, stirring most of the time, until the juices have almost evaporated. Add a squeeze of lemon juice and season to taste with salt and pepper. Stir in the parsley and cook for a further minute.

Transfer the sautéed mushrooms to a warmed serving dish and serve piping hot or warm. Accompany with chunks or slices of crusty bread for mopping up the garlic cooking juices.

WILD MUSHROOMS SUCH AS BOLETUSES OR CHANTERELLES CAN BE USED IN PLACE OF CULTIVATED MUSHROOMS. COURGETTES MAY ALSO BE PREPARED IN THE SAME WAY, WITH A FINELY CHOPPED SMALL ONION FRIED IN THE OIL UNTIL LIGHTLY BROWNED BEFORE ADDING THE GARLIC.

STUFFED CHERRY TOMATOES

SERVES 8
as part of a tapas meal

24 cherry tomatoes

Anchovy and Olive Filling

50 g/1³/₄ oz canned
anchovy fillets in olive oil

8 pimiento-stuffed green
olives, finely chopped

2 large hard-boiled eggs,
finely chopped

pepper

OR

Crab Mayonnaise Filling

170 g/6 oz canned
crabmeat, drained

4 tbsp mayonnaise

1 tbsp chopped fresh
flat-leaved parsley

salt and pepper

OR

*Black Olive and Caper
Filling*

12 stoned black olives

3 tbsp capers

6 tbsp Aïoli (see page 92)

salt and pepper

Several different choices of filling have been given in this recipe, so make a decision before you begin, or, of course, you could make a selection of each. Simply cut the filling quantities to stuff the corresponding number of tomatoes.

If necessary, cut and discard a very thin slice from the stalk end of each tomato to make the bases flat and stable. Cut a thin slice from the smooth end of each tomato and discard. Using a serrated knife or teaspoon, loosen the pulp and seeds of each and scoop out, discarding the flesh. Turn the scooped-out tomatoes upside down on kitchen paper and leave to drain for 5 minutes.

To make the anchovy and olive filling, drain the anchovies, reserving the oil for later, chop finely and put in a bowl. Add the olives and hard-boiled eggs. Pour in a trickle of oil from the drained anchovies to moisten the mixture, season with pepper (don't add salt to season as the anchovies will provide enough) and mix well together.

To make the crab mayonnaise filling, put the crabmeat, mayonnaise and parsley in a bowl and mix well together. Season the filling to taste with salt and pepper.

To make the black olive and caper filling, put the olives and capers on kitchen paper to drain them well, then chop finely and put in a bowl. Add the Aïoli and mix well together. Season the filling to taste with salt and pepper.

Fill a piping bag fitted with a 2-cm/³/₄-inch plain nozzle with the filling of your choice and use to pack the filling into the hollow tomato shells. Store the tomatoes in the refrigerator until ready to serve.

CHERRY TOMATOES ARE MADE FOR JUST ONE MOUTHFUL BUT, IF YOU PREFER, LARGER TOMATOES COULD BE STUFFED WITH THE FILLINGS. THE QUANTITIES GIVEN IN THE RECIPE WILL FILL ABOUT 10 MEDIUM TOMATOES.

GARLIC FRIED BREAD & CHORIZO

SERVES 6–8
as part of a tapas meal

200 g/7 oz chorizo sausage, outer casing removed

4 thick slices 2-day-old country bread

Spanish olive oil, for shallow-frying

3 garlic cloves, finely chopped

2 tbsp chopped fresh flat-leaved parsley

paprika, to garnish

Cut the chorizo sausage into 1-cm/^{1}/$_2$-inch thick slices and cut the bread, with its crusts still on, into 1-cm/^{1}/$_2$-inch cubes. Add sufficient olive oil to a large, heavy-based frying pan so that it generously covers the base. Heat the oil, add the garlic and fry for 30 seconds–1 minute, or until lightly browned.

Add the bread cubes to the pan and fry, stirring all the time, until golden brown and crisp. Add the chorizo slices and fry for 1–2 minutes, or until hot. Using a slotted spoon, remove the bread cubes and chorizo from the pan and drain well on kitchen paper.

Turn the fried bread and chorizo into a warmed serving bowl, add the chopped parsley and toss together. Garnish the dish with a sprinkling of paprika and serve warm. Accompany with cocktail sticks so that a piece of sausage and a cube of bread can be speared together for eating.

CHOOSE A SOFT CHORIZO SAUSAGE FOR THIS RECIPE AS, ALTHOUGH IT WILL NOT HAVE BEEN CURED FOR A LONG PERIOD, THE SOFT VARIETIES USUALLY CONTAIN A HIGH PROPORTION OF FAT, WHICH MAKES THEM VERY GOOD FOR COOKING. AS AN ALTERNATIVE TO CHORIZO, YOU COULD USE THICKLY CUT SERRANO HAM OR EVEN GARLIC SAUSAGE.

A SALAD OF MELON, CHORIZO & ARTICHOKES

SERVES 8
as part of a tapas meal

12 small globe artichokes

juice of 1/2 lemon

2 tbsp Spanish olive oil

1 small orange-fleshed melon, such as cantaloupe

200 g/7 oz chorizo sausage, outer casing removed

few sprigs of fresh tarragon or flat-leaved parsley, to garnish

Dressing

3 tbsp Spanish extra virgin olive oil

1 tbsp red wine vinegar

1 tsp prepared mustard

1 tbsp chopped fresh tarragon

salt and pepper

To prepare the artichokes, cut off the stalks. With your hands, break off the toughest outer leaves at the base until the tender inside leaves are visible. Using a pair of scissors, cut the spiky tips off the leaves. Using a sharp knife, pare the dark green skin from the base and down the stem. As you prepare them, brush the cut surfaces of the artichokes with lemon juice to prevent discoloration. Alternatively, you could fill a bowl with cold water to which you have added a little lemon juice, and immerse the artichokes in the acidulated water to stop discolouration. Carefully remove the choke (the mass of silky hairs) by pulling it out with your fingers or by scooping it out with a spoon. It is very important to remove all the choke as the little barbs, if eaten, can irritate the throat. However, if you are using very young artichokes, you do not need to worry about removing the choke and you can include the stalk too, well scraped, as it will be quite tender. Cut the artichokes into quarters and brush them again with lemon juice.

Heat the olive oil in a large, heavy-based frying pan, then add the prepared artichokes and fry, stirring frequently, for 5 minutes, or until the artichoke leaves are golden brown. Remove from the pan, transfer to a large serving bowl and leave to cool.

To prepare the melon, cut in half and scoop out the seeds with a spoon. Cut the flesh into bite-sized cubes. Add to the cooled artichokes. Cut the chorizo into bite-sized chunks and add to the melon and artichokes.

To make the dressing, put all the ingredients in a small bowl and whisk together. Just before serving, pour the dressing over the prepared salad ingredients and toss together. Serve the salad garnished with tarragon or parsley sprigs.

IF YOU ARE UNABLE TO FIND FRESH ARTICHOKES, YOU COULD USE 400 G/14 OZ CANNED ARTICHOKE HEARTS. SIMPLY DRAIN THE JUICES FROM THE CAN AND SLICE THE ARTICHOKE HEARTS IN HALF OR IN QUARTERS. AS A VARIATION, YOU COULD USE SERRANO HAM, CUT IN ONE THICK PIECE RATHER THAN SLICED, INSTEAD OF THE CHORIZO.

AUBERGINE & PEPPER DIP

SERVES 6–8
as part of a tapas meal

2 large aubergines

2 red peppers

4 tbsp Spanish olive oil

2 garlic cloves, roughly chopped

grated rind and juice of ¹/₂ lemon

1 tbsp chopped fresh coriander, plus extra sprigs to garnish

¹/₂–1 tsp paprika

salt and pepper

bread or toast, to serve

Preheat the oven to 190°C/375°F/Gas Mark 5. Prick the skins of the aubergines and peppers all over with a fork and brush with about 1 tablespoon of the olive oil. Put on a baking tray and bake in the oven for 45 minutes, or until the skins are beginning to turn black, the flesh of the aubergine is very soft and the peppers are deflated.

When the vegetables are cooked, put them in a bowl and immediately cover tightly with a clean, damp tea towel. Alternatively, you can put the vegetables in a polythene bag. Leave them for about 15 minutes until they are cool enough to handle.

When the vegetables have cooled, cut the aubergines in half lengthways, carefully scoop out the flesh and discard the skin. Cut the aubergine flesh into large chunks. Remove and discard the stem, core and seeds from the peppers and cut the flesh into large pieces.

Heat the remaining olive oil in a large, heavy-based frying pan, add the aubergine flesh and pepper pieces and fry for 5 minutes. Add the garlic and fry for a further 30 seconds.

Turn all the contents of the frying pan on to kitchen paper to drain, then transfer to the bowl of a food processor. Add the lemon rind and juice, the chopped coriander, the paprika, and salt and pepper according to taste, and blend until a speckled purée is formed.

Turn the aubergine and pepper dip into a serving bowl. Serve warm, at room temperature, or leave to cool for 30 minutes, then chill in the refrigerator for at least 1 hour and serve cold. Garnish with coriander sprigs and accompany with thick slices of bread or toast for dipping.

INSTEAD OF COOKING THE AUBERGINES AND PEPPERS IN THE OVEN, THEY CAN BE COOKED UNDER THE GRILL UNTIL THE SKINS ARE CHARRED ALL OVER. THEY DO, HOWEVER, NEED TO BE TURNED FREQUENTLY AND THEY WILL TAKE ABOUT 10 MINUTES. THIS DIP IS ALSO VERY GOOD SERVED WITH COLD MEATS.

SIZZLING
CHILLI PRAWNS

SERVES 8
as part of a tapas meal

500 g/1 lb 2 oz raw tiger prawns, in their shells

1 small fresh red chilli

6 tbsp Spanish olive oil

2 garlic cloves, finely chopped

pinch of paprika

salt

crusty bread, to serve

To prepare the prawns, pull off their heads. With your fingers, peel off their shells, leaving the tails intact. Using a sharp knife, make a shallow slit along the underside of each prawn, then pull out the dark vein and discard. Rinse the prawns under cold water and dry well on kitchen paper.

Cut the chilli in half lengthways, remove the seeds and finely chop the flesh. It is important either to wear gloves or to wash your hands very thoroughly after chopping chillies as their juices can cause irritation to sensitive skin, especially around the eyes, nose or mouth.

Whatever you do, don't rub your eyes after touching the cut flesh of the chilli.

Heat the olive oil in a large, heavy-based frying pan or flameproof casserole until quite hot, then add the garlic and fry for 30 seconds. Add the prawns, chilli, paprika and a pinch of salt and fry for 2–3 minutes, stirring all the time, until the prawns turn pink and begin to curl.

Serve the prawns in the cooking dish, still sizzling. Accompany with cocktail sticks, to spear the prawns, and chunks or slices of crusty bread to mop up the aromatic cooking oil.

THE POINT OF THIS DISH IS THAT THE PAN IS BROUGHT TO THE TABLE AND THE PRAWNS ARE SERVED REALLY HOT, HENCE THEIR NAME. THE OIL SHOULD STILL BE SIZZLING, AND SO IT IS USUALLY BROUGHT TO THE TABLE WITH A PLATE OF BREAD PERCHED ON TOP.

FRIED MANCHEGO CHEESE

SERVES 6–8
as part of a tapas meal

200 g/7 oz Manchego cheese

3 tbsp plain flour

salt and pepper

1 egg

1 tsp water

85 g/3 oz fresh white or brown breadcrumbs

sunflower oil, for deep-frying

Slice the cheese into triangular shapes about 2 cm/³/4 inch thick or alternatively into cubes measuring about the same size. Put the flour in a polythene bag and season with salt and pepper to taste. Break the egg into a shallow dish and beat together with the water. Spread the breadcrumbs on to a plate.

Toss the cheese pieces in the flour so that they are evenly coated, then dip the cheese in the egg mixture. Finally, dip the cheese in the breadcrumbs so that the pieces are coated on all sides. Transfer to a large plate and store in the refrigerator until you are ready to serve them.

Just before serving, heat about 2.5 cm/1 inch of the sunflower oil in a large, heavy-based frying pan or heat the oil in a deep fryer to 180–190°C/350–375°F, or until a cube of bread browns in 30 seconds. Add the cheese pieces, in batches of about 4 or 5 pieces so that the temperature of the oil does not drop, and fry for 1–2 minutes, turning once, until the cheese is just beginning to melt and they are golden brown on all sides. Do make sure that the oil is hot enough otherwise the coating on the cheese will take too long to become crisp and the cheese inside may ooze out.

Using a slotted spoon, remove the fried cheese from the frying pan or deep fryer and drain well on kitchen paper. Serve the fried cheese pieces hot, accompanied by cocktail sticks on which to spear them.

MANCHEGO CHEESE IS SPAIN'S MOST FAMOUS CHEESE. IT IS SOLD AT VARIOUS STAGES OF ITS MATURITY, ALTHOUGH THE MOST WIDELY AVAILABLE IS THE FIRM, FULL-FLAVOURED HARD CHEESE, AS OPPOSED TO THE SOFT, MILD YOUNG CHEESE WHICH IS RARELY FOUND OUTSIDE SPAIN. OTHER CHEESES WORK EQUALLY WELL HERE, SUCH AS CHEDDAR, MOZZARELLA OR EVEN A FIRM GOAT'S CHEESE.

CHORIZO IN RED WINE

SERVES 6
as part of a tapas meal

200 g/7 oz chorizo
sausage

200 ml/7 fl oz Spanish
red wine

2 tbsp brandy (optional)

chopped fresh flat-leaved
parsley, to garnish

crusty bread, to serve

Before you begin, bear in mind that this dish is best if prepared the day before you are planning to serve it.

Using a fork, prick the chorizo sausage in 3 or 4 places. Put it in a large saucepan and pour in the wine. Bring the wine to the boil, then reduce the heat, cover and simmer gently for 15–20 minutes. Transfer the chorizo and wine to a bowl or dish, cover, and leave the sausage to marinate in the wine for 8 hours or overnight.

The next day, remove the chorizo from the bowl or dish and reserve the wine for later. Remove the outer casing from the chorizo and cut the sausage into 5-mm/¼-inch slices. Place

the slices in a large, heavy-based frying pan or flameproof serving dish.

If you are adding the brandy, pour it into a small saucepan and heat gently. Pour the brandy over the chorizo slices, stand well back and set alight. When the flames have died down, shake the pan gently, add the reserved wine to the pan and cook over a high heat until almost all of the wine has evaporated.

Serve the chorizo in red wine piping hot, in the dish in which it was cooked, sprinkled with parsley to garnish. Accompany with chunks or slices of bread to mop up the juices and provide cocktail sticks to spear the pieces of chorizo.

IT IS ALSO FUN TO MAKE THIS DISH WITH SMALL, INDIVIDUAL CHORIZO SAUSAGES. PREPARE THEM IN EXACTLY THE SAME WAY BUT, AFTER REMOVING THEIR OUTER CASING, KEEP THEM WHOLE RATHER THAN SLICING. YOU CAN ALSO USE CIDER IN PLACE OF THE RED WINE, SINCE IT IS OFTEN USED IN THE NORTH OF SPAIN.

Fresh fish and shellfish are the pride of Spanish tapas. They are eaten in vast quantities and you only have to pay a visit to a Spanish fish market to see the array of different varieties. Prawns are popular all over Spain and you will find a dish or two on almost all tapas menus. In the north you will often find mussels, while in the south fried fish is a favourite tapa. Recipes such as Lime-drizzled Prawns, Mussels with Herb & Garlic Butter, and Calamares can be found in this chapter.

The popularity of prawns is very much in evidence in the older-style Spanish tapas bars. One reason for this is that, apart from the

PART TWO
FRESH FROM THE SEA

occasional fork, cutlery is not involved in eating tapas, so prawns are peeled with enthusiasm and the shells discarded on the floor along with lemon pips, cocktail sticks and paper napkins. A covering of sawdust on the floor is often provided for this very reason!

Just one word on cooking the fish – try not to overcook it or it will become tasteless and dry rather than remaining tender.

The selection of recipes in this chapter can be used for various occasions. As many tapas dishes are in fact similar to starters, they all, without exception, make smart, elegant first courses. Simply halve the number of servings that the recipe indicates.

TUNA WITH PIMIENTO-STUFFED OLIVES

SERVES 6
as part of a tapas meal

2 fresh tuna steaks, weighing about 250 g/9 oz in total and about 2.5 cm/1 inch thick

5 tbsp Spanish olive oil

3 tbsp red wine vinegar

4 sprigs of fresh thyme, plus extra to garnish

1 bay leaf

salt and pepper

2 tbsp plain flour

1 onion, finely chopped

2 garlic cloves, finely chopped

85 g/3 oz pimiento-stuffed green olives, sliced

crusty bread, to serve

Don't get caught out with this recipe – the tuna steaks need to be marinated, so remember to start preparing the dish the day before you are going to serve it. Remove the skin from the tuna steaks, then cut the steaks in half along the grain of the fish. Cut each half into 1-cm/1/2-inch thick slices against the grain.

Put 3 tablespoons of the olive oil and the vinegar in a large, shallow, non-metallic dish. Strip the leaves from the sprigs of thyme and add these to the dish with the bay leaf and salt and pepper to taste. Add the prepared strips of tuna, cover the dish and leave to marinate in the refrigerator for 8 hours or overnight.

The next day, put the flour in a polythene bag. Remove the tuna strips from the marinade,

reserving the marinade for later, add them to the bag of flour and toss well until they are lightly coated.

Heat the remaining olive oil in a large, heavy-based frying pan. Add the onion and garlic and gently fry for 5–10 minutes, or until softened and golden brown. Add the tuna strips to the pan and fry for 2–5 minutes, turning several times, until the fish becomes opaque. Add the reserved marinade and olives to the pan and cook for a further 1–2 minutes, stirring, until the fish is tender and the sauce has thickened.

Serve the tuna and olives piping hot, garnished with thyme sprigs. Accompany with chunks or slices of crusty bread for mopping up the sauce.

NOW THAT TUNA CAN EASILY BE BOUGHT FRESH, IT IS A REAL TREAT. IT HAS A FIRM FLESH AND A SUPERB FLAVOUR. ONCE COOKED – GRILLED, FRIED, BAKED OR BRAISED – YOU CAN EAT IT AS A STEAK OR EXACTLY THE SAME WAY AS YOU WOULD CANNED TUNA.

COD & CAPER CROQUETTES

THE SECRET OF COOKING CROQUETTES SUCCESSFULLY IS TO CHILL THE MIXTURE IN THE REFRIGERATOR BEFORE FRYING. YOU WILL THEN FIND THAT THEY DON'T DISINTEGRATE WHEN PUT IN THE HOT OIL. AS A MATTER OF INTEREST, SPAIN IS THE WORLD'S LARGEST PRODUCER OF CAPERS!

MAKES 12

350 g/12 oz white fish fillets, such as cod, haddock or monkfish

300 ml/10 fl oz milk

salt and pepper

4 tbsp olive oil or 55 g/ 2 oz butter

55 g/2 oz plain flour

4 tbsp capers, roughly chopped

1 tsp paprika

1 garlic clove, crushed

1 tsp lemon juice

3 tbsp chopped fresh flat-leaved parsley, plus extra sprigs to garnish

1 egg, beaten

55 g/2 oz fresh white breadcrumbs

1 tbsp sesame seeds

sunflower oil, for deep-frying

lemon wedges, to garnish

mayonnaise, to serve

Put the fish fillets in a large, heavy-based frying pan. Pour in the milk and season to taste with salt and pepper. Bring to the boil, then reduce the heat, cover the pan and simmer gently for 8–10 minutes, or until the fish flakes easily when tested with a fork. Using a fish slice, remove the fish fillets from the pan. Pour the milk into a jug and reserve for later. Flake the fish, removing and discarding the skin and bones.

Heat the olive oil or butter in a saucepan. Stir in the flour to form a paste and cook gently, stirring, for 1 minute. Remove the saucepan from the heat and gradually stir in the reserved milk until smooth. Return to the heat and slowly bring to the boil, stirring all the time, until the mixture thickens.

Remove the saucepan from the heat, add the flaked fish and beat until the mixture is smooth.

Add the capers, paprika, garlic, lemon juice and parsley and mix well together. Season the mixture to taste with salt and pepper. Spread the fish mixture in a dish and leave until cool, then cover and put in the refrigerator for 2–3 hours or overnight.

When the fish mixture has chilled, pour the beaten egg on to a plate. Put the breadcrumbs and sesame seeds on a separate plate, mix together and spread out. Divide the fish mixture into 12 equal-sized portions. Then, with lightly floured hands, form each portion into a sausage shape, measuring about 7.5 cm/3 inches in length. Dip the croquettes, one at a time, in the beaten egg, roll in the breadcrumb mixture to coat them. Place on a plate and chill in the refrigerator for about 1 hour.

To cook the croquettes, heat the oil in a deep fryer to 180–190°C/350–375°F, or until a cube of bread browns in 30 seconds. Add the croquettes, in batches, and fry for 3 minutes, or until golden brown and crispy. Remove from the pan with a slotted spoon and drain well on kitchen paper.

Serve piping hot, garnished with lemon wedges and parsley sprigs and accompanied by a bowl of mayonnaise for dipping.

MONKFISH, ROSEMARY & BACON SKEWERS

MAKES 12

350 g/12 oz monkfish tail or 250 g/9 oz monkfish fillet

12 stalks of fresh rosemary

3 tbsp Spanish olive oil

juice of 1/2 small lemon

1 garlic clove, crushed

salt and pepper

6 thick back bacon rashers

lemon wedges, to garnish

Aïoli (see page 92), to serve

If using monkfish tail, cut either side of the central bone with a sharp knife and remove the flesh to form 2 fillets. Slice the fillets in half lengthways, then cut each fillet into 12 bite-sized chunks to give a total of 24 pieces. Put the monkfish pieces in a large bowl.

To prepare the rosemary skewers, strip the leaves off the stalks and reserve them, leaving a few leaves at one end.

For the marinade, finely chop the reserved leaves and whisk together in a bowl with the olive oil, lemon juice, garlic and salt and pepper to taste. Add the monkfish pieces and toss until

coated in the marinade. Cover and leave to marinate in the refrigerator for 1–2 hours.

Cut each bacon rasher in half lengthways, then in half widthways, and roll up each piece. Thread 2 pieces of monkfish alternately with 2 bacon rolls on to the prepared rosemary skewers.

Preheat the grill, griddle or barbecue. If you are cooking the skewers under an overhead grill, arrange them on the grill pan so that the leaves of the rosemary skewers protrude from the grill and therefore do not catch fire during cooking. Grill the monkfish and bacon skewers for 10 minutes, turning from time to time and basting with any remaining marinade, or until cooked. Serve hot, garnished with lemon wedges for squeezing over them and accompanied by a bowl of Aïoli in which to dip the monkfish skewers.

MONKFISH IS IDEAL FOR SKEWERS BECAUSE OF ITS FIRM TEXTURE, BUT OTHER FIRM-FLESHED FISH, SUCH AS COD, SWORDFISH OR TUNA, WOULD MAKE IDEAL ALTERNATIVES. INSTEAD OF USING ROSEMARY STALKS, YOU CAN USE THE MORE TRADITIONAL METAL SKEWERS OR WOODEN BAMBOO SKEWERS. THE LATTER SHOULD BE PRE-SOAKED IN COLD WATER FOR 30 MINUTES TO PREVENT THEM FROM BURNING.

CALAMARES

SERVES 6
as part of a tapas meal

450 g/1 lb prepared squid
(see Note)

plain flour, for coating

sunflower oil, for deep-
frying

salt

lemon wedges, to garnish

Aïoli (see page 92), to
serve

Slice the squid into 1-cm/¹/₂-inch rings and halve the tentacles if large. Rinse and dry well on kitchen paper so that they do not spit during cooking. Dust the squid rings with flour so that they are lightly coated. Do not season the flour, as Spanish cooks will tell you that seasoning squid with salt before cooking toughens it. They should know!

Heat the sunflower oil in a deep fryer to 180–190°C/350–375°F, or until a cube of bread browns in 30 seconds. Carefully add the squid rings, in batches so that the temperature of the oil does not drop, and fry for 2–3 minutes, or until golden brown and crisp all over, turning several times. Do not overcook as the squid will become tough and rubbery rather than moist and tender.

Using a slotted spoon, remove the fried squid from the deep fryer and drain well on kitchen paper. Keep warm in a warm oven while you fry the remaining squid rings.

Sprinkle the fried squid rings with salt and serve piping hot, garnished with lemon wedges for squeezing over them. Accompany with a bowl of Aïoli in which to dip the calamares.

SQUID IS AVAILABLE ALREADY PREPARED AND SLICED INTO RINGS. IF YOU NEED TO PREPARE THE SQUID YOURSELF, HOLD THE BODY IN ONE HAND AND PULL ON THE HEAD AND TENTACLES WITH THE OTHER. THE BODY CONTENTS WILL COME AWAY TOO AND CAN BE DISCARDED. CUT OFF THE EDIBLE TENTACLES JUST ABOVE THE EYES AND DISCARD THE HEAD. REMOVE THE INK SACS FROM THE HEAD CAREFULLY SO THAT YOU DO NOT PIERCE THEM AND KEEP IF YOU WANT THEM FOR ANOTHER DISH. FINALLY, REMOVE THE BACKBONE AND PEEL OFF THE THIN, DARK OUTER SKIN.

SARDINES MARINATED IN SHERRY VINEGAR

SERVES 6
as part of a tapas meal

12 small fresh sardines

175 ml/6 fl oz Spanish olive oil

4 tbsp sherry vinegar

2 carrots, cut into julienne strips

1 onion, thinly sliced

1 garlic clove, crushed

1 bay leaf

salt and pepper

4 tbsp chopped fresh flat-leaved parsley

few sprigs of fresh dill, to garnish

lemon wedges, to serve

If it has not already been done, clean the fish by scraping the scales off with a knife, being careful not to cut the skin. The choice is yours whether you then leave the heads and tails on or cut them off and discard. Slit along the belly of each fish and remove the innards under cold running water. Then, dry each fish well on kitchen paper.

Heat 4 tablespoons of the olive oil in a large, heavy-based frying pan. Add the sardines and fry for 10 minutes, or until browned on both sides. Using a fish slice, very carefully remove the sardines from the pan and transfer to a large, shallow, non-metallic dish that will hold the sardines in a single layer.

Gently heat the remaining olive oil and the sherry vinegar in a large saucepan, add the carrot strips, onion, garlic and bay leaf and simmer gently for 5 minutes until softened. Season the vegetables to taste with salt and pepper. Allow the mixture to cool slightly, then pour the marinade over the sardines.

Cover the dish and allow the sardines to cool before transferring to the refrigerator. Leave to marinate for about 8 hours or overnight, spooning the marinade over the sardines occasionally, although there is no necessity to get up in the middle of the night! Return the sardines to room temperature before serving, sprinkle with parsley and garnish with dill sprigs. Serve with lemon wedges.

FRESH TROUT OR SALMON FILLETS CAN BE GIVEN THE SAME TREATMENT, BUT INSTEAD OF FRYING THE FISH, IT IS BETTER TO STEAM THE FILLETS FOR 5 MINUTES, OR UNTIL TENDER. WHEN COOKED, SLICE EACH FILLET IN HALF LENGTHWAYS. YOU WILL NEED 6 FISH FILLETS IN TOTAL FOR THIS RECIPE.

FRESH **SALMON IN MOJO SAUCE**

SERVES 8
as part of a tapas meal

4 fresh salmon fillets,
weighing about 750 g/
1 lb 10 oz in total

salt and pepper

3 tbsp Spanish olive oil

1 fresh flat-leaved parsley
sprig, to garnish

Mojo Sauce

2 garlic cloves, peeled

2 tsp paprika

1 tsp ground cumin

5 tbsp Spanish extra virgin
olive oil

2 tbsp white wine vinegar

salt

To prepare the mojo sauce, put the garlic, paprika and cumin in the bowl of a food processor fitted with the metal blade and, using a pulsing action, blend for 1 minute to mix well together. With the motor still running, add 1 tablespoon of the olive oil, drop by drop, through the feeder tube. When it has been added, scrape down the sides of the bowl with a spatula, then very slowly continue to pour in the oil in a thin, steady stream, until all the oil has been added and the sauce has slightly thickened. Add the vinegar and blend for a further 1 minute. Season the sauce with salt to taste.

To prepare the salmon, remove the skin, cut each fillet in half widthways, then cut lengthways into 2-cm/³⁄₄-inch thick slices, discarding any bones. Season the pieces of fish to taste with salt and pepper.

Heat the olive oil in a large, heavy-based frying pan. When hot, add the pieces of fish and fry for about 10 minutes, depending on its thickness, turning occasionally until cooked and browned on both sides.

Transfer the salmon to a warmed serving dish, drizzle over some of the mojo sauce and serve hot, garnished with parsley and accompanied by the remaining sauce in a small serving bowl.

MOJO SAUCE IS ALSO KNOWN AS CANARY ISLAND RED SAUCE, AFTER ITS PLACE OF ORIGIN. WHEN SERVED WITHOUT THE PAPRIKA BUT WITH FINELY CHOPPED FRESH CORIANDER AND PARSLEY LEAVES, IT IS KNOWN AS CANARY ISLAND GREEN SAUCE. IT IS ALSO GOOD DRIZZLED OVER BOILED NEW POTATOES.

SCALLOPS IN SAFFRON SAUCE

SERVES 8
as part of a tapas meal

150 ml/5 fl oz dry white wine

150 ml/5 fl oz fish stock

large pinch of saffron strands

900 g/2 lb shelled scallops, preferably large ones

salt and pepper

3 tbsp Spanish olive oil

1 small onion, finely chopped

2 garlic cloves, finely chopped

150 ml/5 fl oz double cream

squeeze of lemon juice

chopped fresh flat-leaved parsley, to garnish

crusty bread, to serve

Put the wine, fish stock and saffron in a saucepan and bring to the boil. Reduce the heat, cover and simmer gently for 15 minutes.

Meanwhile, remove and discard from each scallop the tough, white muscle that is found opposite the coral, and separate the coral from the scallop. Slice the scallops vertically into thick slices, including the corals if they are present. Dry the scallops well on kitchen paper, then season to taste with salt and pepper.

Heat the olive oil in a large, heavy-based frying pan. Add the onion and garlic and fry for 5 minutes, or until softened and lightly browned. Add the sliced scallops to the pan and fry gently for 5 minutes, stirring occasionally, or until they just turn opaque. The secret is not to overcook the scallops, as otherwise they will become tough and rubbery.

Using a slotted spoon, remove the scallops from the pan and transfer to a warmed plate. Add the saffron liquid to the pan, bring to the boil and boil rapidly until reduced to about half. Reduce the heat and gradually stir in the cream, just a little at a time. Simmer gently until the sauce thickens.

Return the scallops to the pan and simmer for 1–2 minutes just to heat them through. Add a squeeze of lemon juice and season to taste with salt and pepper. Serve the scallops hot, garnished with the parsley and accompanied by chunks or slices of crusty bread to mop up the saffron sauce.

SHELLED SCALLOPS ARE AVAILABLE, BOTH FRESH AND FROZEN, FROM SUPERMARKETS AND FISHMONGERS. SHOULD YOU BUY THEM FROM A FISHMONGER, ASK IF YOU CAN HAVE SOME SHELLS, AS THEY MAKE ATTRACTIVE SERVING DISHES. YOU WILL NEED TO SCRUB THEM CLEAN BEFORE USE.

LIME-DRIZZLED PRAWNS

SERVES 6
as part of a tapas meal

4 limes

12 raw king prawns, in
their shells

3 tbsp Spanish olive oil

2 garlic cloves, finely
chopped

splash of dry sherry

salt and pepper

4 tbsp chopped fresh
flat-leaved parsley

Grate the rind and squeeze out the juice from
2 of the limes. Cut the remaining 2 limes into
wedges and reserve for later.

To prepare the prawns, remove the legs,
leaving the shells and tails intact. Using a sharp
knife, make a shallow slit along the underside
of each prawn, then pull out the dark vein and
discard. Rinse the prawns under cold water
and dry well on kitchen paper.

Heat the olive oil in a large, heavy-based
frying pan, then add the garlic and fry for
30 seconds. Add the prawns and fry for
5 minutes, stirring from time to time, or until
they turn pink and begin to curl. Mix in the lime
rind, juice and a splash of sherry to moisten,
then stir well together.

Transfer the cooked prawns to a serving dish,
season to taste with salt and pepper and
sprinkle over the parsley. Serve piping hot,
accompanied by the reserved lime wedges for
squeezing over the prawns.

THIS DISH CAN ALSO BE
PREPARED WITH COOKED
FRESH OR FROZEN PRAWNS.
MAKE SURE THAT YOU DRY
THEM VERY WELL ON
KITCHEN PAPER BEFORE USING
AND, AS THEY ARE ALREADY
COOKED, ADD THEM TO THE
PAN FOR JUST 1–2 MINUTES,
SIMPLY TO HEAT THEM
THROUGH.

MUSSELS WITH HERB & GARLIC BUTTER

SERVES 8
as part of a tapas meal

800g/1 lb 12 oz fresh
mussels, in their shells

splash of dry white wine

1 bay leaf

85 g/3 oz butter

35 g/1¼ oz fresh white or
brown breadcrumbs

4 tbsp chopped fresh
flat-leaved parsley, plus
extra sprigs to garnish

2 tbsp snipped fresh
chives

2 garlic cloves, finely
chopped

salt and pepper

lemon wedges, to serve

Clean the mussels by scrubbing or scraping the shells and pulling out any beards that are attached to them. Discard any with broken shells and any that refuse to close when tapped. Put the mussels in a colander and rinse well under cold running water. Preheat the oven to 230°C/450°F/Gas Mark 8.

Put the mussels in a large saucepan and add a splash of wine and the bay leaf. Cook, covered, over a high heat for 5 minutes, shaking the saucepan occasionally, or until the mussels are opened. Drain the mussels and discard any that remain closed.

Shell the mussels, reserving one half of each shell. Arrange the mussels, in their half shells, in a large, shallow, ovenproof serving dish.

Melt the butter and pour into a small bowl. Add the breadcrumbs, parsley, chives, garlic and salt and pepper to taste and mix well together. Leave until the butter has set slightly. Using your fingers or 2 teaspoons, take a large pinch of the herb and butter mixture and use to fill each mussel shell, pressing it down well. Chill the filled mussels in the refrigerator until ready to serve.

To serve, bake the mussels in the oven for 10 minutes, or until hot. Serve immediately, garnished with parsley sprigs and accompanied by lemon wedges for squeezing over them.

DUE TO THE LACK OF LUSH PASTURELAND IN MOST OF SPAIN, DAIRY CATTLE ARE NOT EXTENSIVELY RAISED AND THEREFORE OIL, AS OPPOSED TO BUTTER, IS MORE COMMONLY USED IN COOKING. NEVERTHELESS, BUTTER IS OCCASIONALLY USED, AS ILLUSTRATED IN THIS RECIPE.

CRAB TARTLETS

MAKES 24

1 tbsp Spanish olive oil

1 small onion, finely chopped

1 garlic clove, finely chopped

splash of dry white wine

2 eggs

150 ml/5 fl oz milk or single cream

175 g/6 oz canned crabmeat, drained

55 g/2 oz Manchego or Parmesan cheese, grated

2 tbsp chopped fresh flat-leaved parsley

pinch of freshly grated nutmeg

salt and pepper

sprigs of fresh dill, to garnish

Pastry

350 g/12 oz plain flour, plus extra for dusting

pinch of salt

175 g/6 oz butter

2 tbsp cold water

OR

500 g/1 lb 2 oz ready-made shortcrust pastry

Preheat the oven to 190°C/375°F/Gas Mark 5. To prepare the crabmeat filling, heat the olive oil in a saucepan, add the onion and fry for 5 minutes, or until softened but not browned. Add the garlic and fry for a further 30 seconds. Add a splash of wine and cook for 1–2 minutes, or until most of the wine has evaporated.

Lightly whisk the eggs in a large mixing bowl, then whisk in the milk or cream. Add the crabmeat, cheese and parsley, and the onion mixture. Season the mixture with nutmeg and salt and pepper to taste and mix well together.

To prepare the pastry if you are making it yourself, mix the flour and salt together in a large mixing bowl. Add the butter, cut into small pieces, and rub in until the mixture resembles fine breadcrumbs. Gradually stir in enough of the water to form a firm dough. Alternatively, the pastry could be made in a food processor.

On a lightly floured work surface, thinly roll out the pastry. Using a plain, round 7-cm/2³/4-inch cutter, cut the pastry into 18 rounds. Gently pile the trimmings together, roll out again, then

You ONLY HAVE TO LOOK ALONG THE SHELVES OF A SPANISH SUPERMARKET TO SEE THE NUMEROUS VARIETIES OF CANNED FISH THAT ARE AVAILABLE. ON THAT NOTE, CANNED SALMON OR TUNA COULD EASILY BE USED IN THIS RECIPE IN PLACE OF THE CRABMEAT.

cut out a further 6 rounds. Use to line 24 × 4-cm/1¹/2-inch tartlet tins. Carefully spoon the crabmeat mixture into the pastry cases, taking care not to overfill them.

Bake the tartlets in the oven for 25–30 minutes, or until golden brown and set. Serve the crab tartlets hot or cold, garnished with fresh dill sprigs.

This chapter includes some of Spain's most popular tapas dishes. Eggs are an instant tapa on their own and a selection of tapas dishes, particularly in the south of Spain, would be incomplete without Devilled Eggs. A wedge of the thick potato omelette, Tortilla Española, has to be Spain's most popular egg dish.

Cubes of cheese are another instant tapa. Spain produces many cheeses, but the one that is the most easy to obtain outside Spain is Manchego, which is made from sheep's milk. If you are unable to find it, then use freshly cut Italian Parmesan cheese.

Meat dishes are included here too and, although meat has never been plentiful in Spain, pork is a popular meat, as are cured serrano ham and chicken. The Chicken Livers in Sherry Sauce is a firm favourite! Chorizo, flavoured with paprika and garlic, is Spain's favourite sausage, and can be eaten cold or fried, baked or cooked in a sauce.

PART THREE EGG, CHEESE AND MEAT MORSELS

If possible, serve these meat tapas dishes in small, earthenware bowls, just as they are seen on every bar counter in Spain. These dishes retain the heat or cold well, so will keep your tapas dish at the correct temperature. If you don't have any, don't worry! Ordinary serving dishes will serve the purpose equally well. These meat tapas also make delicious light lunch or supper dishes. Simply halve the number that the recipe suggests it will serve and accompany with some good fresh country bread to mop up the juices.

TORTILLA ESPANOLA

SERVES 8
as part of a tapas meal

450 g/1 lb waxy potatoes

425 ml/15 fl oz Spanish
olive oil

2 onions, chopped

2 large eggs

salt and pepper

sprigs of fresh flat-leaved
parsley, to garnish

Peel the potatoes, cut into small cubes or wedges, then put on a clean tea towel and dry well. Heat the olive oil in a large, heavy-based or non-stick frying pan. Add the potato pieces and onions, then reduce the heat and fry the potatoes, stirring frequently so that they do not clump together, for 20 minutes, or until they are tender but not browned. The secret of success is to cook the potatoes for a long time so that they absorb the flavour of the oil and are cooked but not browned or crisp, and do not fall apart. They are in fact almost boiled rather than fried.

Meanwhile, beat the eggs lightly in a large bowl and season well with salt and pepper. Place a sieve over a large bowl.

When the potatoes and onions are cooked, drain them into the sieve so that the bowl catches the oil. Reserve the oil for future use.

THIS IS SPAIN'S CLASSIC TAPAS DISH (AS WELL AS THE STAPLE FOOD FOR A PICNIC) AND IS MADE WITH POTATO, ONION AND EGG. OTHER INGREDIENTS CAN BE ADDED, SUCH AS HAM, BACON, CHEESE, MUSHROOMS, RED OR GREEN PEPPERS, ASPARAGUS AND ARTICHOKE HEARTS, BUT THE SPANISH PREFER TO KEEP IT PLAIN.

When the potatoes and onions are well drained, gently stir them into the beaten eggs.

Wipe the frying pan clean or wash it if necessary to prevent the tortilla from sticking. Heat 2 tablespoons of the reserved olive oil in the pan. When hot, add the egg and potato mixture, reduce the heat and cook for 3–5 minutes, or until the underside is just set. Use a spatula to push the potatoes down into the egg so that they are completely submerged and keep loosening the tortilla from the base of the pan to stop it sticking.

To cook the second side of the tortilla, cover it with a plate and hold the plate in place with the other hand. Drain off the oil in the pan, then quickly turn the pan upside down so that the tortilla falls on to the plate. Return the frying pan to the heat and add a little more of the reserved oil to it if necessary. Slide the tortilla, cooked side uppermost, back into the pan and fry for a further 3–5 minutes, or until set underneath. The tortilla is cooked when it is firm and crisp on the outside but still slightly runny in the centre.

Slide the tortilla on to a serving plate and leave to stand for about 15 minutes. Serve it warm or cold, cut into small squares, fingers or wedges and garnished with parsley sprigs.

DEVILLED EGGS

MAKES 16

8 large eggs

2 whole pimientos
(sweet red peppers) from
a jar or can

8 green olives

5 tbsp mayonnaise

8 drops Tabasco sauce

large pinch cayenne
pepper

salt and pepper

paprika, for dusting

sprigs of fresh dill, to
garnish

To cook the eggs, put them in a saucepan, cover with cold water and slowly bring to the boil. Immediately reduce the heat to very low, cover and simmer gently for 10 minutes. As soon as the eggs are cooked, drain them and put under cold running water until they are cold. By doing this quickly, it will prevent a black ring from forming around the egg yolk. Gently tap the eggs to crack the eggshells and leave them until cold. When cold, crack the shells all over and remove them.

Using a stainless steel knife, halve the eggs lengthways, then carefully remove the yolks. Put the yolks in a nylon sieve, set over a bowl, and rub through, then mash them with a wooden spoon or fork. If necessary, rinse the egg whites under cold water and dry very carefully.

Put the pimientos on kitchen paper to dry well, then chop them finely, reserving a few strips. Finely chop the olives. If you are going to pipe the filling into the eggs, you need to chop both these ingredients very finely so that they will go through a 1-cm/½-inch nozzle. Add the chopped pimientos and most of the chopped olives to the mashed egg yolks, reserving 16 larger pieces to garnish. Add the mayonnaise, mix well together, then add the Tabasco sauce, cayenne pepper and salt and pepper to taste.

For a grand finale, put the egg yolk mixture into a piping bag fitted with a 1-cm/½-inch plain nozzle and pipe the mixture into the hollow egg whites. Alternatively, for a simpler finish, use a teaspoon to spoon the prepared filling into each egg half.

Arrange the eggs on a serving plate. Add a small strip of the reserved pimientos and a piece of olive to the top of each stuffed egg. Dust with a little paprika and garnish with dill sprigs.

IN THE SOUTH OF SPAIN, THE SELECTION OF DISHES SERVED IN TAPAS BARS WOULD BE CONSIDERED INCOMPLETE WITHOUT THE INCLUSION OF THESE DEVILLED EGGS AND TORTILLA ESPAÑOLA (SEE PAGE 54). AS A VARIATION, YOU COULD USE ROLLED, CANNED ANCHOVY FILLETS TO GARNISH EACH EGG.

CHEESE & OLIVE EMPANADILLAS

MAKES 26

85 g/3 oz firm or soft cheese (see Note)

85 g/3 oz stoned green olives

55 g/2 oz sun-dried tomatoes in oil, drained

50 g/1¾ oz canned anchovy fillets, drained

pepper

55 g/2 oz sun-dried tomato paste

plain flour, for dusting

500 g/1 lb 2 oz ready-made puff pastry, thawed if frozen

beaten egg, to glaze

Preheat the oven to 200°C/400°F/Gas Mark 6. Cut the cheese into small dice measuring about 5 mm/¼ inch. Chop the olives, sun-dried tomatoes and anchovies into pieces about the same size as the cheese. Put all the chopped ingredients in a bowl, season with pepper to taste and gently mix together. Stir in the sun-dried tomato paste.

On a lightly floured work surface, thinly roll out the puff pastry. Using a plain, round 8-cm/3¼-inch cutter, cut into 18 rounds. Gently pile the trimmings together, roll out again, then cut out a further 8 rounds. Using a teaspoon, put a little of the prepared filling equally in the centre of each of the pastry rounds.

Dampen the edges of the pastry with a little water, then bring up the sides to completely

cover the filling and pinch the edges together with your fingers to seal them. With the tip of a sharp knife, make a small slit in the top of each pastry. You can store the pastries in the refrigerator at this stage until you are ready to bake them.

Place the pastries on to dampened baking trays and brush each with a little beaten egg to glaze. Bake in the oven for 10–15 minutes, or until golden brown, crisp and well risen. Serve the empanadillas piping hot, warm or cold.

SINCE THERE ARE NOT MANY SPANISH CHEESES AVAILABLE OUTSIDE SPAIN, YOU CAN CHOOSE TO MAKE THESE PASTRIES WITH MANCHEGO, CHEDDAR, GRUYÈRE, GOUDA, MOZZARELLA OR A FIRM GOAT'S CHEESE. LARGE VERSIONS OF THESE EMPANADILLAS ARE KNOWN AS EMPANADAS.

CHEESE PUFFS WITH FIERY TOMATO SALSA

SERVES 8
as part of a tapas meal

70 g/2¹/₂ oz plain flour

50 ml/2 fl oz Spanish olive oil

150 ml/5 fl oz water

2 eggs, beaten

55 g/2 oz Manchego, Parmesan, Cheddar, Gouda or Gruyère cheese, finely grated

¹/₂ tsp paprika

salt and pepper

sunflower oil, for deep-frying

Fiery Tomato Salsa

2 tbsp Spanish olive oil

1 small onion, finely chopped

1 garlic clove, crushed

splash of dry white wine

400 g/14 oz canned chopped tomatoes

1 tbsp tomato purée

¹/₄–¹/₂ tsp red chilli pepper flakes

dash of Tabasco sauce

pinch of sugar

salt and pepper

To make the salsa, heat the olive oil in a saucepan, add the onion and fry for 5 minutes, or until softened but not browned. Add the garlic and fry for a further 30 seconds. Add the wine and allow to bubble, then add all the remaining salsa ingredients to the saucepan and simmer, uncovered, for 10–15 minutes, or until a thick sauce is formed. Spoon into a serving bowl and set aside until ready to serve.

Meanwhile, prepare the cheese puffs. Sift the flour on to a plate or sheet of greaseproof paper. Put the olive oil and water in a saucepan and slowly bring to the boil. As soon as the water boils, remove the saucepan from the heat and quickly tip in the flour all at once. Using a

wooden spoon, beat the mixture well until it is smooth and leaves the sides of the saucepan.

Leave the mixture to cool for 1–2 minutes, then gradually add the eggs, beating hard after each addition and keeping the mixture stiff. Add the cheese and paprika, season to taste with salt and pepper and mix well together. You can store the mixture in the refrigerator at this stage until you are ready to fry the cheese puffs.

Just before serving the cheese puffs, heat the sunflower oil in a deep fryer to 180–190°C/350–375°F, or until a cube of bread browns in 30 seconds. Drop teaspoonfuls of the prepared mixture, in batches, into the hot oil and fry for 2–3 minutes, turning once, or until golden brown and crispy. They should rise to the surface of the oil and puff up. Drain well on kitchen paper.

Serve the puffs piping hot, accompanied by the fiery salsa for dipping and cocktail sticks to spear the puffs.

THESE CRISP LITTLE CHEESE PUFFS ARE LIGHT AND FLUFFY, AND ALTHOUGH IN THIS RECIPE THEY ARE SERVED WITH A SALSA, THEY CAN, IF PREFERRED, SIMPLY BE ACCOMPANIED BY SMALL PICKLED CUCUMBERS. SERVE THESE SPEARED ON COCKTAIL STICKS SO THAT A PICKLED CUCUMBER AND A CHEESE PUFF CAN BE EATEN TOGETHER.

CHORIZO EMPANADILLAS

MAKES 12

125 g/4¹/₂ oz chorizo sausage, outer casing removed

plain flour, for dusting

250 g/9 oz ready-made puff pastry, thawed if frozen

beaten egg, to glaze

paprika, to garnish

Preheat the oven to 200°C/400°F/Gas Mark 6. Cut the chorizo sausage into small dice measuring about 1 cm/¹/₂ inch square.

On a lightly floured work surface, thinly roll out the puff pastry. Using a plain, round 8-cm/3¹/₄-inch cutter, cut into rounds. Gently pile the trimmings together, roll out again, then cut out further rounds to produce 12 in total. Put about a teaspoon of the chopped chorizo on to each of the pastry rounds.

Dampen the edges of the pastry with a little water, then fold one half over the other half to completely cover the chorizo. Seal the edges together with your fingers. Using the prongs of a fork, press against the edges to give a decorative finish and seal them further. With the tip of a sharp knife, make a small slit in the side of each pastry. You can store the pastries in the refrigerator at this stage until you are ready to bake them.

Place the pastries onto dampened baking trays and brush each with a little beaten egg to glaze. Bake in the oven for 10–15 minutes, or until golden brown and puffed. Using a small sieve, lightly dust the top of each empanadilla with a little paprika to garnish. Serve the chorizo empanadillas hot or warm.

A TAPAS MEAL WOULD NOT BE COMPLETE WITHOUT THE INCLUSION OF CHORIZO! IN THIS RECIPE IT IS ENCASED IN PUFF PASTRY AND MAKES A DELICIOUS ACCOMPANIMENT TO A GLASS OF CHILLED WHITE WINE. THE EMPANADILLAS ARE PARTICULARLY EASY TO PREPARE – IN FACT SOMETHING A CHILD MIGHT LIKE TO MAKE. JUST WATCH THAT THEY DON'T EAT ALL THE CHORIZO BEFORE IT REACHES THE OVEN!

TINY SPANISH MEATBALLS IN ALMOND SAUCE

SERVES 6–8
as part of a tapas meal

55 g/2 oz white or brown bread, crusts removed

3 tbsp water

450 g/1 lb fresh lean pork mince (see Note)

1 large onion, finely chopped

1 garlic clove, crushed

2 tbsp chopped fresh flat-leaved parsley, plus extra to garnish

1 egg, beaten

freshly grated nutmeg

salt and pepper

flour, for coating

2 tbsp Spanish olive oil

squeeze of lemon juice

crusty bread, to serve

Almond Sauce

2 tbsp Spanish olive oil

25 g/1 oz white or brown bread

115 g/4 oz blanched almonds

2 garlic cloves, finely chopped

150 ml/5 fl oz dry white wine

salt and pepper

425 ml/15 fl oz vegetable stock

To prepare the meatballs, put the bread in a bowl, add the water and leave to soak for 5 minutes. With your hands, squeeze out the water and return the bread to the dried bowl. Add the pork, onion, garlic, parsley and egg, then season generously with grated nutmeg and a little salt and pepper. Knead the ingredients well together to form a smooth mixture.

Spread some flour on a plate. With floured hands, shape the meat mixture into about 30 equal-sized balls, then roll each meatball again in flour until coated.

Heat the olive oil in a large, heavy-based frying pan, add the meatballs, in batches so that they do not overcrowd the pan, and fry for 4–5 minutes, or until browned on all sides. Using a slotted spoon, remove the meatballs from the pan and set aside.

To make the almond sauce, heat the olive oil in the same frying pan in which the meatballs were fried. Break the bread into pieces, add to the pan with the almonds and fry gently, stirring frequently, until the bread and almonds are golden brown. Add the garlic and fry for a further 30 seconds, then pour in the wine and boil for 1–2 minutes. Season to taste with salt and pepper and allow to cool slightly.

Transfer the almond mixture to a food processor. Pour in the vegetable stock and blend the mixture until smooth. Return the sauce to the frying pan.

Carefully add the fried meatballs to the almond sauce and simmer for 25 minutes, or until the meatballs are tender. Taste the sauce and season with salt and pepper if necessary.

Transfer the cooked meatballs and almond sauce to a warmed serving dish, then add a squeeze of lemon juice to taste and sprinkle with chopped parsley to garnish. Serve piping hot, accompanied by chunks or slices of crusty bread for mopping up the almond sauce.

MINCED PORK, OR A COMBINATION OF PORK AND VEAL, IS THE MOST TRADITIONAL MEAT USED IN SPAIN TO MAKE THESE MEATBALLS, BUT THERE IS NO REASON WHY YOU COULD NOT USE LAMB OR BEEF MINCE, IF PREFERRED.

MINIATURE PORK BROCHETTES

MAKES 12

450 g/1 lb lean boneless pork (see Note)

3 tbsp Spanish olive oil, plus extra for oiling (optional)

grated rind and juice of 1 large lemon

2 garlic cloves, crushed

2 tbsp chopped fresh flat-leaved parsley, plus extra to garnish

1 tbsp ras-el-hanout spice blend (see Note)

salt and pepper

The brochettes are marinated overnight, so remember to do this in advance in order that they are ready when you need them. Cut the pork into pieces about 2 cm/³/₄ inch square and put in a large, shallow, non-metallic dish that will hold the pieces in a single layer.

To prepare the marinade, put all the remaining ingredients in a bowl and mix well together. Pour the marinade over the pork and toss the meat in it until well coated. Cover the dish and leave to marinate in the refrigerator for 8 hours or overnight, stirring the pork 2–3 times.

You can use wooden or metal skewers to cook the brochettes and for this recipe you will need about 12 × 15-cm/6-inch skewers. If you are using wooden ones, soak them in cold water for about 30 minutes prior to using. This helps to stop them burning and the food sticking to them during cooking. Metal skewers simply need to be greased, and flat ones should be used in preference to round ones to prevent the food on them falling off.

Preheat the grill, griddle or barbecue. Thread about 3 marinated pork pieces, leaving a little space between each piece, on to each prepared skewer. Cook the brochettes for 10–15 minutes or until tender and lightly charred, turning several times and basting with the remaining marinade during cooking. Serve the pork brochettes piping hot, garnished with parsley.

ALTHOUGH USUALLY MADE WITH PORK IN SPAIN, THESE BROCHETTES ARE OF ARAB ORIGIN, AND WOULD BE MADE USING LAMB; BOTH ARE DELICIOUS. THE RAS-EL-HANOUT SPICE BLEND, FOUND IN DELICATESSENS AND LARGER SUPERMARKETS, CONSISTS OF GALANGAL, ROSEBUDS, BLACK PEPPERCORNS, GINGER, CARDAMOM, NIGELLA, CAYENNE, ALLSPICE, LAVENDER, CINNAMON, CASSIA, CORIANDER, MACE, NUTMEG AND CLOVES!

CHICKEN IN LEMON AND GARLIC

SERVES 6–8
as part of a tapas meal

4 large skinless, boneless chicken breasts

5 tbsp Spanish olive oil

1 onion, finely chopped

6 garlic cloves, finely chopped

grated rind of 1 lemon, finely pared rind of 1 lemon and juice of both lemons

4 tbsp chopped fresh flat-leaved parsley, plus extra to garnish

salt and pepper

lemon wedges and crusty bread, to serve

THERE ARE SEVERAL VARIATIONS TO THIS POPULAR, QUICK AND EASY-TO-PREPARE TAPAS DISH. TRY, FOR EXAMPLE, USING CHICKEN WINGS OR, IN PLACE OF THE CHICKEN, USE SLICES OF FRESH RABBIT, TURKEY OR PORK.

Using a sharp knife, slice the chicken breasts widthways into very thin slices. Heat the olive oil in a large, heavy-based frying pan, add the onion and fry for 5 minutes, or until softened but not browned. Add the garlic and fry for a further 30 seconds.

Add the sliced chicken to the pan and fry gently for 5–10 minutes, stirring from time to time, until all the ingredients are lightly browned and the chicken is tender.

Add the grated lemon rind and the lemon juice and let it bubble. At the same time, deglaze the pan by scraping and stirring all the bits on the base of the pan into the juices with a wooden spoon. Remove the pan from the heat, stir in the parsley and season to taste with salt and pepper.

Transfer the chicken in lemon and garlic, piping hot, to a warmed serving dish. Sprinkle with the pared lemon rind, garnish with the parsley and serve with lemon wedges for squeezing over the chicken, accompanied by chunks or slices of crusty bread for mopping up the lemon and garlic juices.

CRISPY CHICKEN & HAM CROQUETTES

MAKES 8

4 tbsp olive oil or 55 g/
2 oz butter

4 tbsp plain flour

200 ml/7 fl oz milk

115 g/4 oz cooked
chicken, minced

55 g/2 oz serrano or
cooked ham, very finely
chopped

1 tbsp chopped fresh
flat-leaved parsley, plus
extra sprigs to garnish

small pinch of freshly
grated nutmeg

salt and pepper

1 egg, beaten

55 g/2 oz day-old white
breadcrumbs

sunflower oil, for
deep-frying

Aïoli (see page 92),
to serve

Heat the olive oil or butter in a saucepan. Stir in the flour to form a paste and cook gently for 1 minute, stirring constantly. Remove the saucepan from the heat and gradually stir in the milk until smooth. Return to the heat and slowly bring to the boil, stirring all the time, until the mixture boils and thickens.

Remove the saucepan from the heat, add the minced chicken and beat until the mixture is smooth. Add the chopped ham, parsley and nutmeg and mix well together. Season the mixture to taste with salt and pepper. Spread the chicken mixture in a dish and leave for 30 minutes until cool, then cover and put in the refrigerator for 2–3 hours or overnight. Don't be tempted to miss out this stage, as chilling the croquettes helps to stop them falling apart when they are cooked.

When the chicken mixture has chilled, pour the beaten egg onto a plate and spread the breadcrumbs out on a separate plate. Divide the chicken mixture into 8 equal-sized portions. With dampened hands, form each portion into a cylindrical shape. Dip the croquettes, one at a time, in the beaten egg, then roll in the breadcrumbs to coat them. Place on a plate and chill in the refrigerator for about 1 hour.

To cook the croquettes, heat the oil in a deep fryer to 180–190°C/350–375°F, or until a cube of bread browns in 30 seconds. Add the croquettes, in batches to prevent the temperature of the oil dropping, and fry for 5–10 minutes, or until golden brown and crispy. Remove from the pan with a slotted spoon and drain well on kitchen paper.

Serve the chicken and ham croquettes piping hot, garnished with parsley sprigs and accompanied by a bowl of Aïoli for dipping.

THESE CRISPY CROQUETTES ARE ANOTHER VERY POPULAR TAPAS SERVED ALL OVER SPAIN AND COME IN AN ENORMOUS VARIETY OF FLAVOURS, INCLUDING COD & CAPER CROQUETTES (SEE PAGE 34), AND IN ALL SHAPES AND SIZES, FROM ROUND AND OVAL TO FLAT AND CYLINDRICAL, AS THEY ARE IN THIS RECIPE.

CHICKEN LIVERS IN SHERRY SAUCE

SERVES 6
as part of a tapas meal

450 g/1 lb chicken livers

2 tbsp Spanish olive oil

1 small onion, finely
chopped

2 garlic cloves, finely
chopped

100 ml/3$^{1}/_{2}$ fl oz dry
Spanish sherry

salt and pepper

2 tbsp chopped fresh
flat-leaved parsley

crusty bread or toast,
to serve

If necessary, trim the chicken livers, cutting away any ducts and gristle, then cut them into small, bite-sized pieces.

Heat the olive oil in a large, heavy-based frying pan. Add the onion and fry for 5 minutes, or until softened but not browned. Add the garlic and fry for a further 30 seconds.

Add the chicken livers to the pan and fry for 2–3 minutes, stirring all the time, until they are firm and have changed colour on the outside but are still pink and soft in the centre. Using a slotted spoon, lift the chicken livers from the pan, transfer them to a large, warmed serving dish or several smaller ones and keep warm.

Add the sherry to the pan, increase the heat and let it bubble for 3–4 minutes to evaporate the alcohol and reduce slightly. At the same time, deglaze the pan by scraping and stirring all the bits on the base of the pan into the sauce

with a wooden spoon. Season the sauce to taste with salt and pepper.

Pour the sherry sauce over the chicken livers and sprinkle over the parsley. Serve piping hot, accompanied by chunks or slices of crusty bread or toast to mop up the sherry sauce.

THIS TAPAS DISH IS OFTEN SERVED IN ANDALUCIA'S TAPAS BARS AND IS EQUALLY POPULAR MADE WITH LAMB'S OR CALF'S KIDNEYS. FOR A VARIATION, YOU COULD ADD SOME HALVED OR QUARTERED MUSHROOMS AND/OR A TABLESPOON OF DRAINED CAPERS OR CHOPPED GREEN OLIVES.

There are many tapas dishes that are based on vegetables, which in Spain are treated with loving care. The Spanish serve tapas vegetable dishes when the vegetables are in season and you should do the same. The Roasted Asparagus with Mountain Ham dish should, for example, appear on your table in spring!

A dish that deserves a mention but doesn't warrant a recipe is for small green peppers that are slit at their base end, their insides rubbed with a pinch of salt, then slowly fried in shallow olive oil until very tender. They are then picked up by their stems and eaten whole, discarding the seeds. Another vegetable dish that should not be overlooked is the Russian Salad served in tapas bars all over Spain. Do not think of the once-popular canned vegetable concoction of

PART FOUR THE VEGETABLE CONNECTION

the same name, since it is only the name that has any resemblance. It can, incidentally, also be served as a meal in its own right.

Potato dishes are particularly popular tapas and there are several here to choose from – the Baby Potatoes with Aïoli being a particular favourite. Aïoli, the garlic mayonnaise from Catalonia, is the recipe that you will turn to time and time again when serving tapas dishes! It is a tapa classic and appears on every tapas menu. While we're on the subject, it can be written as one word as it is here or sometimes as ai-l-oli. The Spaniards themselves can't even agree!

BROAD BEANS WITH SERRANO HAM

SERVES 6–8
as part of a tapas meal

55 g/2 oz serrano or
Parma ham, pancetta or
rindless smoked streaky
bacon

115 g/4 oz chorizo
sausage, outer casing
removed

4 tbsp Spanish olive oil

1 onion, finely chopped

2 garlic cloves, finely
chopped

splash of dry white wine

450 g/1 lb frozen broad
beans, thawed, or about
1.3 kg/3 lb fresh broad
beans in their pods,
shelled to give 450 g/1 lb

1 tbsp chopped fresh mint
or dill, plus extra to
garnish

pinch of sugar

salt and pepper

Using a sharp knife, cut the ham, pancetta or bacon into small strips. Cut the chorizo into 2-cm/³/₄-inch cubes. Heat the olive oil in a large, heavy-based frying pan or flameproof dish that has a lid. Add the onion and fry for 5 minutes, or until softened and beginning to brown. If you are using pancetta or bacon, add it with the onion. Add the garlic and fry for a further 30 seconds.

Pour the wine into the pan, increase the heat and let it bubble to evaporate the alcohol, then reduce the heat. Add the broad beans, ham, if using, and the chorizo and fry for 1–2 minutes, stirring all the time to coat in the oil.

Cover the pan and let the beans simmer very gently in the oil, stirring from time to time, for 10–15 minutes, or until the beans are tender. It may be necessary to add a little water to the pan during cooking, so keep an eye on it and add a splash if the beans appear to become too dry. Stir in the mint or dill and sugar. Season the dish with salt and pepper, but taste first as you may find that it does not need any salt.

Transfer the broad beans to a large, warmed serving dish, several smaller ones or individual plates and serve piping hot, garnished with chopped mint or dill.

BOTH FRESH AND DRIED BROAD BEANS ARE HIGHLY REGARDED IN SPAIN. IN THIS RECIPE YOU CAN USE FRESH OR, IF MORE CONVENIENT, FROZEN BROAD BEANS, BUT IF YOU CHOOSE THE LATTER MAKE SURE THAT THEY ARE BABY ONES, AS THEY ARE MORE TENDER. IF YOU HAVE TIME, YOU CAN REMOVE THE SKINS FROM THE BEANS TO REVEAL THE SOFT, BRIGHT-GREEN BEAN INSIDE, BUT IT IS A TIME-CONSUMING TASK!

STUFFED PIMIENTOS

MAKES 7–8

185 g/6¹/₂ oz canned or bottled whole pimientos del piquillo (chargrilled sweet red peppers)

salt and pepper

fresh herb sprigs, to garnish

Curd Cheese and Herb Filling

225 g/8 oz curd cheese

1 tsp lemon juice

1 garlic clove, crushed

4 tbsp chopped fresh flat-leaved parsley

1 tbsp chopped fresh mint

1 tbsp chopped fresh oregano

salt and pepper

OR

Tuna Mayonnaise Filling

200 g/7 oz canned tuna steak in olive oil, drained

5 tbsp mayonnaise

2 tsp lemon juice

2 tbsp chopped fresh flat-leaved parsley

salt and pepper

OR

Goat's Cheese and Olive Filling

50 g/1³/₄ oz stoned black olives, finely chopped

200 g/7 oz soft goat's cheese

1 garlic clove, crushed

salt and pepper

There is actually a choice of fillings provided in this recipe – the final decision is yours. Lift the peppers from the jar, reserving the oil for later.

To make the curd cheese and herb filling, put the curd cheese in a bowl and add the lemon juice, garlic, parsley, mint and oregano. Mix well together. Season to taste with salt and pepper.

To make the tuna and mayonnaise filling, put the tuna in a bowl and add the mayonnaise, lemon juice and parsley. Add 1 tablespoon of the reserved oil from the jar of pimientos and mix well. Season to taste with salt and pepper.

To make the goat's cheese and olive filling, put the olives in a bowl and add the goat's cheese, garlic and 1 tablespoon of the reserved oil from the jar of pimientos. Mix well together. Season to taste with salt and pepper.

Using a teaspoon, heap the filling of your choice into each pimiento. Put in the refrigerator and chill for at least 2 hours until firm.

To serve the pimientos, arrange them on a serving plate and, if necessary, wipe with kitchen paper to remove any of the filling that has spread over the skins. Garnish with herb sprigs.

MAKE SURE THAT YOU BUY WHOLE PEPPERS, NOT SLICED. PIMIENTO IS SIMPLY THE SPANISH WORD FOR PEPPER, BUT OUTSIDE SPAIN THE WORD IS USED TO REFER TO RED PEPPERS THAT ARE COOKED, PEELED AND SOLD IN JARS OR CANS. IF YOU CAN'T FIND PIMIENTOS DEL PIQUILLO, LOOK FOR A JAR OF PEPPADEW PEPPERS FROM SOUTH AFRICA. THIS RECIPE WILL FILL ABOUT 36 PEPPADEW PEPPERS.

GREEN BEANS WITH PINE KERNELS

SERVES 8
as part of a tapas meal

2 tbsp Spanish olive oil

50 g/1¾ oz pine kernels

½–1 tsp paprika

450 g/1 lb green beans

1 small onion, finely chopped

1 garlic clove, finely chopped

salt and pepper

juice of ½ lemon

Heat the oil in a large, heavy-based frying pan, add the pine kernels and fry for about 1 minute, stirring all the time and shaking the pan, until light golden brown. Using a slotted spoon, remove the pine kernels from the pan, drain well on kitchen paper, then transfer to a bowl. Reserve the oil in the frying pan for later. Add the paprika, according to taste, to the pine kernels, stir together until coated, and then set aside.

Top and tail the green beans and remove any strings if necessary. Put the beans in a saucepan, pour over boiling water, return to the boil and cook for 5 minutes, or until tender but still firm. Drain well in a colander.

Reheat the oil in the frying pan, add the onion and fry for 5–10 minutes, or until softened and beginning to brown. Add the garlic and fry for a further 30 seconds.

Add the beans to the pan and cook for 2–3 minutes, tossing together with the onion

until heated through. Season the beans to taste with salt and pepper.

Turn the contents of the pan into a warmed serving dish, sprinkle over the lemon juice and toss together. Scatter over the golden pine kernels and serve hot.

AS A VARIATION TO THE PINE KERNELS, YOU COULD USE FLAKED OR BLANCHED ALMONDS, WHICH SHOULD BE SLICED INTO THIN STRIPS BEFORE FRYING. THEY ARE EQUALLY DELICIOUS – IT IS SIMPLY A MATTER OF PERSONAL PREFERENCE.

ROASTED PEPPER
SALAD

SERVES 8
as part of a tapas meal

3 red peppers

3 yellow peppers

5 tbsp Spanish extra virgin olive oil

2 tbsp dry sherry vinegar or lemon juice

2 garlic cloves, crushed

pinch of sugar

salt and pepper

1 tbsp capers

8 small black Spanish olives

2 tbsp chopped fresh marjoram, plus extra sprigs to garnish

Preheat the grill. Place all the peppers on a wire rack or grill pan and cook under a hot grill for 10 minutes, or until their skins have blackened and blistered all over, turning them frequently, .

Remove the roasted peppers from the heat, put them in a bowl and immediately cover tightly with a clean, damp tea towel.

Alternatively, you can put the peppers in a polythene bag. You will find that the steam helps to soften the skins and makes it easier to remove them. Leave the peppers for about 15 minutes until they are cool enough to handle.

Holding one pepper at a time over a clean bowl, use a sharp knife to make a small hole in the base and gently squeeze out the juices and reserve them. Still holding the pepper over the bowl, carefully peel off the blackened skin with your fingers or a knife and discard it. Cut the peppers in half and remove the stem, core and seeds, then cut each pepper into neat thin strips. Arrange the pepper strips attractively on a serving dish.

To the reserved pepper juices add the olive oil, sherry vinegar, garlic, sugar and salt and pepper to taste. Whisk together until combined. Drizzle the dressing evenly over the salad.

Scatter the capers, olives and chopped marjoram over the salad, garnish with marjoram sprigs and serve at room temperature.

ALTHOUGH CALLED ROASTED PEPPERS, THE PEPPERS FOR THIS RECIPE ARE MORE USUALLY GRILLED THAN ROASTED IN AN OVEN. YOU CAN ALSO SPEAR THEM ON A FORK AND HOLD THEM OVER A GAS FLAME, OR ROAST THEM ON A BARBECUE. RED AND YELLOW PEPPERS HAVE BEEN USED HERE, BUT THERE'S NO REASON WHY YOU CAN'T USE GREEN ONES OR A MIXTURE.

SPANISH SPINACH & TOMATO PIZZAS

MAKES 32

2 tbsp Spanish olive oil, plus extra for brushing and drizzling

1 onion, finely chopped

1 garlic clove, finely chopped

400 g/14 oz canned chopped tomatoes

125 g/4½ oz baby spinach leaves

salt and pepper

25 g/1 oz pine kernels

Bread Dough

100 ml/3½ fl oz warm water

½ tsp easy-blend dried yeast

pinch of sugar

200 g/7 oz strong white flour, plus extra for dusting

½ tsp salt

To make the bread dough, measure the water into a small bowl, sprinkle in the dried yeast and sugar and leave in a warm place for 10–15 minutes, or until frothy.

Meanwhile, sift the flour and salt into a large bowl. Make a well in the centre of the flour and pour in the yeast liquid, then mix together with a wooden spoon. Using your hands, work the mixture until it leaves the sides of the bowl clean.

Turn the dough out on to a lightly floured work surface and knead for 10 minutes, or until smooth and elastic and no longer sticky. Shape into a ball and put it in a clean bowl. Cover with a clean, damp tea towel and leave in a warm place for 1 hour, or until it has risen and doubled in size.

To make the topping, heat the olive oil in a large, heavy-based frying pan. Add the onion and fry for 5 minutes, or until softened but not browned. Add the garlic and fry for a further

30 seconds. Stir in the tomatoes and cook for 5 minutes, letting it bubble and stirring occasionally, until reduced to a thick mixture. Add the spinach leaves and cook, stirring, until they have wilted a little. Season the mixture to taste with salt and pepper.

While the dough is rising, preheat the oven to 200°C/400°F/Gas Mark 6. Brush several baking trays with olive oil. Turn the dough out on to a lightly floured work surface and knead well for 2–3 minutes to knock out the air bubbles. Roll out the dough very, very thinly and, using a 6-cm/2½-inch plain, round cutter, cut out 32 rounds. Place on the prepared baking sheets.

Spread each base with the spinach mixture to cover, then sprinkle the pine kernels over the top. Drizzle a little olive oil over each pizza. Bake in the oven for 10–15 minutes, or until the edges of the dough are golden brown. Serve the spinach and tomato pizzas hot.

ONE ASSOCIATES PIZZAS WITH ITALY, BUT IN FACT THESE SPANISH PIZZAS ARE VERY POPULAR TAPAS DISHES CALLED COCA. THEY WERE TRADITIONALLY MADE FROM A SIMPLE DOUGH OF FLOUR AND WATER, BUT NOW EITHER A BREAD OR PASTRY BASE IS USED. THE TOPPINGS CAN VARY TOO AND MIGHT INCLUDE ANCHOVIES, PEPPERS, HAM, CHORIZO SAUSAGE AND OLIVES, BUT SELDOM CHEESE.

COURGETTE FRITTERS
WITH A DIPPING SAUCE

SERVES 8
as part of a tapas meal

450 g/1 lb baby courgettes

3 tbsp plain flour

1 tsp paprika

1 large egg

2 tbsp milk

sunflower oil, for shallow-frying

coarse sea salt

dipping sauce such as Aïoli (see page 92), Fiery Tomato Salsa (see page 61) or the Pine Kernel Sauce (see below)

Pine Kernel Sauce

100 g/3½ oz pine kernels

1 garlic clove, peeled

3 tbsp Spanish extra virgin olive oil

1 tbsp lemon juice

3 tbsp water

1 tbsp chopped fresh flat-leaved parsley

salt and pepper

If you have chosen to serve the pine kernel sauce with the courgette fritters, then make this first. Put the pine kernels and garlic in a food processor and blend to form a purée. With the motor still running, gradually add the olive oil, lemon juice and water to form a smooth sauce. Stir in the parsley and season to taste with salt and pepper. Turn into a serving bowl.

To prepare the courgettes, cut them on the diagonal into thin slices about 5 mm/¼ inch thick. Put the flour and paprika in a polythene bag and mix together. Beat the egg and milk together in a large bowl.

Add the courgette slices to the flour mixture and toss well together until coated. Shake off the excess flour. Heat the sunflower oil in a large, heavy-based frying pan to a depth of about 1 cm/½ inch. Dip the courgette slices, one at a time, into the egg mixture, then slip them into the hot oil. Fry the courgette slices, in batches of a single layer so that they do not overcrowd the frying pan, for 2 minutes, or until crisp and golden brown.

THE EXACT SAME TREATMENT CAN BE APPLIED TO AUBERGINES, WHILE THE PINE KERNEL SAUCE CAN BE MADE WITH ALMONDS IN EXACTLY THE SAME WAY TOO, IF PREFERRED.

Using a slotted spoon, remove the courgette fritters from the pan and drain on kitchen paper. Continue until all the courgette slices have been fried.

Serve the courgette fritters piping hot, lightly sprinkled with sea salt. Accompany with a bowl of your chosen dipping sauce.

ROASTED ASPARAGUS WITH MOUNTAIN HAM

MAKES 12

2 tbsp Spanish olive oil

6 slices serrano ham

12 asparagus spears

pepper

Aïoli (see page 92), to serve

THE MOST POPULAR SPANISH HAM IS SERRANO, WHICH MEANS MOUNTAIN HAM, BECAUSE IT IS CURED IN THE MOUNTAINS. IT IS THEN AGED FROM SEVERAL MONTHS TO SEVERAL YEARS. IF YOU ARE UNABLE TO OBTAIN IT, YOU COULD USE ITALIAN PARMA HAM OR PROSCIUTTO INSTEAD.

Preheat the oven to 200°C/400°F/Gas Mark 6. Put half the olive oil in a roasting tin that will hold the asparagus spears in a single layer and swirl it around so that it covers the base. Cut each slice of serrano ham in half lengthways.

Trim the ends of the asparagus spears, then wrap a slice of ham around the stem end of each spear. Place the wrapped spears in the prepared roasting tin and lightly brush the ham and asparagus with the remaining olive oil. Season the spears with pepper.

Roast the asparagus spears in the oven for about 10 minutes, depending on the thickness of the asparagus, until tender but still firm. Do not overcook the asparagus spears as it is important that they are still firm, so that you can pick them up with your fingers.

Serve the roasted asparagus with mountain ham piping hot, accompanied by a bowl of Aïoli for dipping.

RUSSIAN SALAD

SERVES 8
as part of a tapas meal

2 eggs

450 g/1 lb baby new
potatoes, quartered

115 g/4 oz fine green
beans, cut into 2.5-cm/
1-inch lengths

115 g/4 oz frozen peas

115 g/4 oz carrots

200 g/7 oz canned tuna
steak in olive oil, drained

2 tbsp lemon juice

8 tbsp mayonnaise

1 garlic clove, crushed

salt and pepper

4 small gherkins, sliced

8 stoned black olives,
halved

1 tbsp capers

1 tbsp chopped fresh
flat-leaved parsley

1 tbsp chopped fresh dill,
plus extra sprigs to
garnish

Put the eggs in a saucepan, cover with cold water and slowly bring to the boil. Immediately reduce the heat to very low, cover and simmer gently for 10 minutes. As soon as the eggs are cooked, drain them and put under cold running water until they are cold. By doing this quickly, you will prevent a black ring from forming around the egg yolk. Gently tap the eggs to crack the eggshells and leave them until cold.

THIS IS ONE OF SPAIN'S MOST POPULAR AND STAPLE TAPAS BAR DISHES. THE VEGETABLES THAT IT CONTAINS VARY, BUT USUALLY THE BASIC SALAD CONSISTS OF POTATOES, CARROTS AND PEAS, AND SOMETIMES TUNA, AS IN THIS RECIPE.

Meanwhile, put the potatoes in a large saucepan of cold, salted water and bring to the boil. Reduce the heat and simmer for 7 minutes, or until just tender. Add the beans and peas to the saucepan for the last 2 minutes of cooking. Drain well, splash under cold running water, then leave the vegetables to cool completely.

Cut the carrots into julienne strips about 2.5 cm/1 inch in length. Flake the tuna into large chunks. When the potatoes, beans and peas are cold, put them in a large bowl. Add the carrot strips and the flaked tuna and very gently toss the ingredients together. Transfer the vegetables and tuna to a salad bowl or large serving dish.

In a jug, stir the lemon juice into the mayonnaise to thin it slightly, then stir in the garlic and season to taste with salt and pepper. Drizzle the mayonnaise dressing over the vegetables and tuna.

Scatter the gherkins, olives and capers into the salad and finally sprinkle over the parsley and dill. You can store the salad in the refrigerator but return to room temperature before serving. Just before serving, crack the shells of the eggs all over and remove them. Slice the eggs into wedges, add them to the salad and garnish with dill sprigs.

BABY POTATOES
WITH AÏOLI

SERVES 6–8
as part of a tapas meal

450 g/1 lb baby new
potatoes

1 tbsp chopped fresh
flat-leaved parsley

salt

Aïoli

1 large egg yolk, at room
temperature

1 tbsp white wine vinegar
or lemon juice

2 large garlic cloves,
peeled

salt and pepper

5 tbsp Spanish extra
virgin olive oil

5 tbsp sunflower oil

To make the Aïoli, put the egg yolk, vinegar or lemon juice, garlic and salt and pepper to taste in the bowl of a food processor fitted with the metal blade and blend well together. With the motor still running, very slowly add the olive oil, then the sunflower oil, drop by drop at first, then, when it begins to thicken, in a slow, steady stream until the sauce is thick and smooth.

For this recipe, the Aïoli should be a little thin so that it coats the potatoes. To insure this, quickly blend in 1 tablespoon water so that it forms the consistency of sauce.

To prepare the potatoes, cut them in half or quarters to make bite-sized pieces. If they are very small, you can leave them whole. Put the potatoes in a large saucepan of cold, salted water and bring to the boil. Reduce the heat and simmer for 7 minutes, or until just tender. Drain well, then turn out into a large bowl.

While the potatoes are still warm, pour over the Aïoli sauce and gently toss the potatoes in it. Adding the sauce to the potatoes while they are still warm will help them to absorb the garlic

flavour. Leave for about 20 minutes to allow the potatoes to marinate in the sauce.

Transfer the potatoes with Aïoli to a warmed serving dish, sprinkle over the parsley and salt to taste and serve warm. Alternatively, the dish can be prepared ahead and stored in the refrigerator, but return it to room temperature before serving.

THE RECIPE GIVEN HERE FOR AÏOLI CONTAINS RAW EGG AND THEREFORE SHOULD BE AVOIDED BY INFANTS, THE ELDERLY, PREGNANT WOMEN, CONVALESCENTS AND ANYONE SUFFERING FROM AN ILLNESS. IF ANY OF THESE CASES APPLIES TO YOU, USE COMMERCIALLY MADE MAYONNAISE AND ADD THE CRUSHED GARLIC TO IT.

FRIED POTATOES WITH
PIQUANT PAPRIKA

SERVES 6
as part of a tapas meal

3 tsp paprika

1 tsp ground cumin

¹/₄–¹/₂ tsp cayenne pepper

¹/₂ tsp salt

450 g/1 lb small old
potatoes, peeled

sunflower oil, for shallow-
frying

sprigs of fresh flat-leaved
parsley, to garnish

Aïoli (see page 92),
to serve (optional)

Put the paprika, cumin, cayenne pepper and salt
in a small bowl and mix well together. Set aside.

Cut each potato into 8 thick wedges. Pour
enough sunflower oil into a large, heavy-based
frying pan so that it comes about 2.5 cm/1 inch
up the sides of the pan. Heat the oil, then add
the potato wedges, preferably in a single layer,
and fry gently for 10 minutes, or until golden
brown all over, turning from time to time,
Remove from the pan with a slotted spoon and
drain on kitchen paper.

Transfer the potato wedges to a large bowl
and, while they are still hot, sprinkle with the
paprika mixture, then gently toss them together
to coat.

Turn the fried potatoes with paprika into one
large, warmed serving dish, several smaller ones
or individual plates and serve hot, garnished with
parsley sprigs. Accompany with a bowl of Aïoli
for dipping, if wished.

A VARIATION IS TO FRY
THE POTATOES AS HERE,
THEN SPOON OVER THE
FIERY TOMATO SALSA
THAT ACCOMPANIES THE
CHEESE PUFFS (SEE PAGE
61), OR SERVE THE SALSA
SEPARATELY FOR DIPPING
THE POTATOES IN. THIS
DISH IS THEN KNOWN
AS PATATAS BRAVAS
(BOLD POTATOES).

INDEX